summer 1985

To. Helen (our friend)

love

From Aunty Mo & Uncle To.
xxx

THE CHILD
WORLD

THE CHILD WORLD.

"Boys and girls get out of bed:
The sun is shining round and red."

· THE · CHILD · WORLD. ·

BY

GABRIEL SETOUN.

AUTHOR OF " BARNCRAIG." "SUNSHINE & HAAR"
ETC.
ILLUSTRATED BY :

CHARLES ROBINSON.

SHAMBHALA
BOULDER
1979

SHAMBHALA PUBLICATIONS, INC.
1123 Spruce Street
Boulder, Colorado 80302

Distributed in the United States by Random House
Printed in the United States of America

LIBRARY OF CONGRESS CATALOGING IN PUBLICATION DATA

Hepburn, Thomas Nicoll
    The child world.
    Reprint of the 1896 ed. published by J. Lane/
The Bodley Head, London.
    I. Robinson, Charles. II. Title.
PR4785.H6C5   1979   821'.8   79-7451
ISBN 0-87773-157-8
ISBN 0-394-73736-9 (Random House)

TO MY MOTHER.

DEAR MOTHER, THESE TO YOU I GIVE,
ALTHOUGH THE WORDS ALREADY LIVE
WITHIN YOUR HEART; FOR YOU HAVE HEARD
MY VERSES, EVERY LINE AND WORD—
YEA, EVEN BEFORE THE THOUGHTS HAD TIME
TO FEEL THEMSELVES AT HOME IN RHYME.
YET THERE IS SOMETHING IN THE LOOK
AND HANDLING OF A PRINTED BOOK
THAT SEEMS TO SAY, "LO, HERE IS CAUGHT
THE SPOKEN WORD OR PASSING THOUGHT
THAT, TOUCHING SOME MYSTERIOUS SPRING,
MAKES ALL THE PAST A LIVING THING."

SO YOU MAY READ, WHO READ BETWEEN
THE LINES BECAUSE YOUR EYES HAVE SEEN
THE CHILD AND HIS CHILD-POEMS GROW.
A POEM OTHERS MAY NOT KNOW
IN GLIMPSES OF THAT JOYOUS LIFE
ALL ON THE SUNNY SHORES OF FIFE.
AND HEAR IN SONG, THOUGH FAINT AND DIM,
AN ECHO OF THE VOICE OF HIM
WHO PASSED AND LEFT US ALL BEFORE
HIS HEART SUMMED HALF THE YEARS HE WORE.

SO, MOTHER DEAR, THIS BOOK TO YOU!
IT MAY BUILD UP THE PAST ANEW
UNTIL AS IN A DREAM YOU SEE
YOUR CHILDREN GATHER ROUND YOUR KNEE
TO LISTEN WHILE A CHAPTER'S READ,
THEN LISP THEIR PRAYERS AND GO TO BED,
AND WHEN THEY'RE SOUND ASLEEP YOU'LL SIT
TO HEAR THE WHILE YOU SEW OR KNIT,
THEIR FATHER'S VOICE SO RICH IN TONE
GIVE VERSE A CHARM NOT ALL ITS OWN;
OR FROM HIS BIG CHAIR READ AGAIN
SOME PASSAGE FROM HIS LOVED MONTAIGNE.

CONTENTS.

HOME AND PLAY.

CONTENTS

12

CONTENTS

FANCIES
AND
PICTURES.

CONTENTS

CONTENTS

THE CHILD WORLD.

HOME
AND
PLAY

BABY'S BIG WORLD.

When the day is nearly done
And the birds-
         have gone to rest,
Baby likes to see the sun
Setting in the-
         golden west.

BABY'S BIG WORLD

So she climbs upon a chair;
  Gazes out with round, blue eyes,
While the sunlight on her hair
  Makes it golden as the skies.

What a big, big world she sees!
  Leafy lanes and winding rills,
Great, green fields and shady trees,
  And far away, the silent hills.

Round about the setting Sun
  Clouds are bidding him good-night;
Baby sees them, every one,
  Glowing in his golden light.

When the clouds are growing dim
  And their gold has changed to red,
Baby sings her evening hymn,
  Lisps her prayer, and goes to bed.

Ere the stars begin to peep
  In the heavens, east and west,
Baby will be sound asleep,
  Like a birdie in its nest.

Round about the setting sun
Clouds are bidding him
Good-night;

Still, perhaps, in dream she sees,
  Leafy lanes, and winding rills,
Great, green fields and shady trees;
  Golden clouds and silent hills.

THE STARS.

O PEN the shutters, put out the light;
    Our gowns are on and our prayers are
        said;
And now we must bid the stars good-night,
  Ere mother haps us up in bed.
        Around the window, one, two, three,
        There's little May and Rob and me.

THE STARS

Father opens the shutters a chink;
  Then lowers the light to let us spy
The stars that stare, and the stars that blink,
  A million lamps in the curtained sky.
     Around the window, hand in hand,
     Three children in their night-gowns stand.

"Yonder's the big one." Little May
  Has seen him first, then Rob, then me.
For I am the oldest and that's the way
  We should watch the stars across the sea.
     Three little children in a row,
     To watch the big one flash and glow.

Then Rob with his face to the window pressed
  Picks out the red one among the white;
For that's the star that Rob likes best
  Because it shines like the harbour light.
     But I point out the row of three
     That stand like May and Rob and me.

Then father, while we stand and gaze,
  Talks of the sky and names the stars;
Mine is Orion's belt; and May's
  Is Sirius; and Rob's is Mars.
     Then into our cosy beds we creep;
     For it's time that children were all asleep.

THE STARS

Good-night, you stars that glint and gleam.
  The shutters are shut; the curtains drawn;
But we'll see you shining down in dream,
  Till you all go out with the rosy dawn.
    Father and mother, a kiss, good-night!
    We'll wake when you let in the morning
    light.

FROM A BEDROOM WINDOW.

DAY by day the shadows grow
    Shorter on the sleeping snow;
Day by day the sunbeams fall
Closer to our garden wall.

When the noon-day sun shall glint
On boxwood, balm, and peppermint;
I'll know that Spring has come, and then
Hurrah! I shall get out again.

MORNING SONG.

Boys and girls get out of bed;
The sun is shining—
round and red
And wakening every—
sleepy head
To go to school—
in the morning.

27

THIS is the way we brush
    our boots;
Make them bright both
    left and right.
This is the way we
    brush our boots
To go to school in the
    morning.

The dewy grass is growing green;
The face of every flower is clean,
And children also should be seen
    As fair for school in the morning.

THIS is the way we wash
   our face,
Leave no speck on
   cheek or neck.
This is the way we
   wash our face
To go to school in the
   morning.

The birds have had their bath, and now
They preen their wings on twig and bough,
And, chirping, tell all children how
   To wash and dress in the morning.

THIS is the way we comb
    our hair.
From the crown we
    shade it down.
This is the way we
    comb our hair
To go to school in the
    morning.

The clouds that looked so black last night
Are sailing now all snowy white;
And boys and girls should be as bright
   To go to school in the morning.

THIS is the way we brush
    our clothes.
Children must beware
    of dust,
This is the way we
    brush our clothes
To go to school in the
    morning.

We'll get our breakfast and away,
With half an hour to run and play,
And so begin a happy day
    In time for school in the morning.

31

ND that is the way that
  boys and girls
Who would be seen
  both neat and clean.
This is the way that
  boys and girls
Prepare for school in
  the morning.

THE END
OF THE SONG

HIDING.

HEN the table-cloth is laid
    And the cups are on the table;
When the tea and toast are made,
    That's a happy time for Mabel.
Stealing to her mother's side,
    In her ear she whispers low,
"When papa comes in I'll hide;
    Do not tell him where I go."

33

HIDING

On her knees upon the floor;
    In below the sofa creeping;
When she hears him at the door
    She pretends that she is sleeping.
"Where is Mabel?" father cries,
    Looking round and round about.
Then he murmurs in surprise,
    "Surely Mabel can't be out."

First he looks behind his chair,
    Then he peers below the table,
Seeking, searching everywhere,
    All in vain for little Mabel.
But at last he thinks he knows;
    And he laughs and shakes his head;
Says to mother, "I suppose
    Mabel has been put to bed."

HIDING

But when he sits down to tea,
  From beneath the sofa creeping,
Mabel climbs upon his knee,
  Claps her hands: "I was not sleeping."
Father whispers, "Where's my girl's
  Very secret hiding place?"
But she only shakes her curls,
  Laughing, smiling in his face

WADING.

SUMMER'S sunny days have come;
   Soft and sweet the wind is blowing;
Bees across the meadow hum
   Where the golden flowers are growing;
Fields and trees are green and fair,
And sunshine's sleeping everywhere.

WADING

O, the sunny summer days,
  When the ripples dance and quiver;
And the sun at noontide lays
  Star-like jewels on the river!
Take your shoes off; wade in here
Where the water's warm and clear.

Listen to the song it sings,
  Ever rippling, ever flowing;
Telling of a thousand things;
  Whence it comes, and whither going;
Singing, like the birds and bees,
Of the wondrous world it sees.

WADING

"Come and I shall bathe your feet,
    Little boys, so warm with playing
In the summer's sultry heat."
    That is what the stream is saying.
Off go jacket, socks, and shoes.
How could any boy refuse?

See the fishes dart about,
    Where a thousand lights are dancing;
Here a minnow, there a trout,
    Like a sword of silver glancing.
Is it hide-and-seek they play
Through the sunny summer day?

WADING

All the wood is filled with sound,
   And the very air is ringing,
Up and down and all around,
   With the songs the birds are singing.
O, the golden summer hours,
When earth's a paradise of flowers!

A LOST WEEK.

I woke one day with wrecks
                    and ships
All topsy-turvy in my head;
And I learned this from
                    mother's lips,
    That I had been a week in bed.

A LOST WEEK

I'd slept so sound though I was ill,
   I had not felt the slightest pain;
Yet mother said I must lie still
   And try to fall asleep again.

To sleep a week was long enough;
   And not to wake, and not to know
That I'd been drinking nasty stuff
   From bottles standing in a row.

Yet still my eyes would not keep wide,
   Even though I heard the shouts of boys
And happy girls at play outside,
   And knew the sound of every voice.

A LOST WEEK

The voices died to a drowsy hum;
 And in the distance, low and deep,
I heard the roll of the engine drum,
 And then—I must have fallen asleep.

SAILING

LITTLE waves, I've brought the boat
    Father made to me;
For I want to see it float
    On the sunny sea.
Take it in your little hands;
Bear it o'er the golden sands.

SAILING

What a pretty boat it is,
   Sail and mast and all!
Father made it just like his,
   Only very small.
And I'm going to call it "Sun,"
For that's the name of father's one.

Little waves, come up and creep
   Round my little boat;
Where the water's ankle-deep
   I shall see it float;
And you'll sing your sweetest song
As it sails and sails along.

SAILING

See, my boatie mounts and dips
   Where you break in foam.
Tell it how the big, big ships
   Sail so far from home;
What they bring, and where they go;
And the thousand things you know.

What is it you sing about?
   Tell me what you say,
Coming in and going out,
   All the summer day.
Whisper to my boat and me
Of the ships far out at sea.

SAILING

Now we're sailing, brave and bold,
   With the gentle breeze;
Seeing islands laid with gold
   Far in foreign seas,
Where the skies are bright and clear,
And it's summer all the year.

Little waves, now must you bring
   My boatie safe to land.
We've listened to the songs you sing
   Creeping o'er the sand.
When I grow older I'll find out
The lovely lands you talk about.

SANTA CLAUS.

IN Spring the sun shines clear and
     bright
And calls us out to run and play,
For, though the winds are cold at night,
  The steaming ground is warm all day.

When Summer brings the birds and bees,
　　And flowers wave o'er all the land,
We want to play among the trees
　　Or dig for sand-eels in the sand.

In Autumn, when the golden sheaves
　　Are ranked about the fields in scores,
And ruddy tints are on the leaves,
　　You do not wish to stay indoors.

SANTA CLAUS

But when the birds and bees are dumb
  And Jack Frost stills the bubbling brooks,
It's then that Santa Claus will come
  And bring you lots of toys and books.

Is it not kind of Santa Claus,
  To think of little girls and boys
When winter nights are long, because
  That's just the time they wish for toys?

WINTER NIGHTS

WHEN winter hangs the hedge with haws
    And whitens hemlocks round the
        park,
We can't get out to play, because,
    As soon as tea is done, it's dark.

It's hard to have to stay at home
    When haws are ripe for hemlock guns;
And so through foreign lands we roam
    To seek the fruits of tropic suns.

Rob folds the screen; and in a nook
  Of dates and figs sits down to feast,
And fills it from his picture book
  With bears and every kind of beast.

I turn the stool up; take my seat
  And sail away to Sinbad-shore,
Where, setting it upon its feet,
  I ride a thousand miles and more.

And to her dolls May's humming low
  The songs that all dolls understand,
While mother knits and doesn't know
  Her chair's the harbour where we'll land.

STORY TIME.

W E get our books when play is
done ;
And May with Bunyan from the shelf
Reads through the pictures one by one
And makes a story up herself.

And Rob slays giants tall as trees
  And witches that infest the land;
Their prisoned princesses he frees
  And fights with dragons hand to hand.

While round the world with Drake I sail,
  And drive the great Armada back;
Or toil through seas of ice, and nail
  Against the Pole the Union Jack.

LULLABY.

HUSH-A-BYE, baby, hush-a-bye, ba !
  Gooing one, cooing one, rest.
The round sun's already asleep in his beddie
  And dreaming a dream of the West.
    Hush-a-bye, hush-a-bye, ba !
      Comfy and cosy,
      Backie and bosie,
    Till morning, sweet morning, ta ta !

LULLABY

Hush-a-bye, baby, hush-a-bye, ba !
 Blinking one, winking one, rest.
The gloaming is falling and curfew is calling
 The little birds home to their nest,
  Hush-a-bye, hush-a-bye, ba !
    Comfy and cosy,
    Feetie and toesie,
  Till morning, bright morning, ta ta !

Hush-a-bye, baby, hush-a-bye, ba !
 Smile you now, while you now sleep.

LULLABY

The starnies are twinkling above you, and sprinkling
Baby stars down on the deep.
Hush-a-bye, hush-a-bye, ba!
Comfy and cosy,
Eyesey and nosey,
Till morning awake thee, ta ta!

MVSIC.

"The world's a very happy place."

THE WORLDS MUSIC.

THE world's a very happy place,
  Where every child should dance and sing,
And always have a smiling face,
  And never sulk for anything.

I waken when the morning's come,
  And feel the air and light alive
With strange sweet music like the hum
  Of bees about their busy hive.

The linnets play among the leaves
  At hide-and-seek, and chirp and sing;
While, flashing to and from the eaves,
  The swallows twitter on the wing.

And twigs that shake, and boughs that sway;
  And tall old trees you could not climb;
And winds that come, but cannot stay,
  Are singing gaily all the time.

From dawn to dark the old mill-wheel
  Makes music, going round and round;
And dusty-white with flour and meal,
  The miller whistles to its sound.

The brook that flows beside the mill,
  As happy as a brook can be,
Goes singing its own song until
  It learns the singing of the sea.

For every wave upon the sands
  Sings songs you never tire to hear,
Of laden ships from sunny lands
  Where it is summer all the year.

THE WORLD'S MUSIC

And if you listen to the rain
   When leaves and birds and bees are dumb,
You hear it pattering on the pane
   Like Andrew beating on his drum.

The coals beneath the kettle croon,
   And clap their hands and dance in glee;
And even the kettle hums a tune
   To tell you when it's time for tea.

The world is such a happy place
   That children, whether big or small,
Should always have a smiling face
   And never, never sulk at all.

THE MUSIC OF
THE SPHERES

WHEN we are fast asleep
    in bed,
  And hear in dream the
    sound of song,
The moon and stars high over-
    head
  Are making music all night
    long.

THE BIRDS' SONGS.

WHAT do the birds all sing about
　　Through the livelong summer day?
The swallows call, "Come out; come out,"
　　And the blackbirds whistle, "To play."

The mavis sings to the rosy dawn
　　Till the sun comes into the sky,
And flings his gold about the lawn
　　Where the dewy diamonds lie.

The lark leaps from the broomy links,
　　And shakes from his wings the dew;
And soaring sings, until he blinks
　　A speck in the azure blue.

63

Then every bower finds a voice;
　And linnets and finches sing;
The grasses dance; the whins rejoice;
　And the bells of the blue-bell ring.

Thus all the day do birdies sing
　Until the light grows dim;
And then the lark on soaring wing
　Towards heaven again must hymn.

The mavis tunes his throat anew,
　And, piping to the west,
He bids the dying day adieu
　And sings a song of rest.

"O what a happy world is ours
　In summer and in spring,
With fields and trees and grass and flowers!"
　That's what the birdies sing.

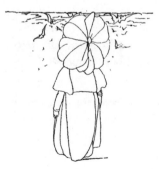

THE WIND'S SONG.

O WINDS that blow across the sea,
   What is the story that you bring?
Leaves clap their hands on every tree
   And birds about their branches sing.

You sing to flowers and trees and birds
   Your sea-songs over all the land.
Could you not stay and whisper words
   A little child might understand?

THE WIND'S SONG

The roses nod to hear you sing;
　But though I listen all the day,
You never tell me anything
　Of father's ship so far away.

Its masts are taller than the trees;
　Its sails are silver in the sun;
There's not a ship upon the seas
　So beautiful as father's one.

With wings spread out it flies so fast
　It leaves the waves all white with foam
Just whisper to me, blowing past,
　If you have seen it sailing home.

I feel your breath upon my cheek,
　And in my hair, and on my brow.
Dear winds, if you could only speak,
　I know what you would tell me now.

THE WIND'S SONG

My father's coming home, you'd say,
  With precious presents, one, two, three;
A shawl for mother, beads for May,
  And eggs and shells for Rob and me.

The winds sing songs where'er they roam;
  The leaves all clap their little hands;
For father's ship is coming home
  With wondrous things from foreign lands.

THE SONG OF THE KETTLE.

WHEN I come hungry home from school,
    I like to hear the kettle sing;
And, seated on the kitchen stool,
    I watch it hanging from the swing.

68

THE SONG OF THE KETTLE

At first it does not say a word;
  And then it tries a chirp or two,
And cheeps a bit, just like a bird
  That wonders what he'll sing to you.

But when its throat is cleared it sings
  Of honey gathered by the bee;
Of cream and jam and all the things
  That you would like to have at tea.

And then I shut my eyes and hear
  The bees hum sweetly as they pass;
And see the lazy cows quite clear
  Go wading ankle deep in grass;

And harvest fields and hill and sky;
  The river and the old mill-wheel,
Where horse and cart go rumbling by
  With swelling sacks of flour and meal.

THE SONG OF THE KETTLE

That's what the kettle sings about;
  I see them like the things you dream;
When all at once its crooked spout
  Sends out a gush of hissing steam.

The lid goes rattling up and down
  And won't keep quiet till mother's come.
And soon the teapot, fat and brown,
  Is singing, and the kettle's dumb.

THE CROWS

WHAT a famous noise there was
    In the morning when I rose!
All the air was hoarse with "caws,"
    And the sky was black with crows.

Hundreds circling round the trees
    Swooped down on a last year's nest;
Rose and scattered, then, like bees,
    Swarmed again and could not rest;

THE CROWS.

THE CROWS

Cawing, cawing all the time;
  Till it grew to one great voice,
And you could not hear the chime
  Of the school-clock for the noise.

Every garden bush has heard,
  Through its tiny twigs and shoots;
And the trees have all been stirred
  Right down to their very roots.

Buds of green on branch and stem
  Glisten in the morning sun;
For the crows have wakened them,
  And they open one by one.

On the hill, last night, there lay
  One white patch from winter-snows.
Now it's melted clean away
  With the cawing of the crows.

And a primrose, too, has heard,
  Peeping out to nod and talk,
From the hedge-roots to a bird,
  Hopping down the garden walk.

THE CROWS

What a famous noise it was!
   To make the trees and bushes hear,
And fields and flowers and leaves, because
   The merry time of spring is near.

THE SEA-SHELL.

H OLD this buckie to your ear—
   What a pleasant sound you hear!

THE SEA-SHELL

All the happy sounds you've heard;
Hum of bee and song of bird;
What the gentle breezes sing
When they wake the flowers in spring;
Songs of trees and running brooks;
Songs you never read in books,
Of the waves and of the tides,
And a thousand more besides;
Songs you've heard the whole year through.
Has this buckie heard them too?

For it's here the breezes bring,
Songs the fields and forests sing.
Here the tides tell twice a day,
Of the wonders far away.
And the buckie drinks its fill
Of their music, lying still,
Listening with open mouth,
To the songs of north and south.

Through its winding whorls they creep,
Where they're singing now in sleep,
A thousand voices never done;
And you hear them all in one.

THE SEA-SHELL

When its song is sad and low,
The tide is going out, you know;
But it shouts with joy and pride,
To welcome in the rising tide.

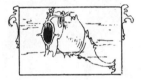

WHAT THE
LEAVES SAY.

I HAVE heard the leaves, and know
   What they speak of, whispering low,
As the breezes come and go.

78

WHAT THE LEAVES SAY

To the South they whisper, " Please
Tell us tales of other trees,
You have seen across the seas."

And the wind, which understands,
Speaks of far off foreign lands,
Till the leaves all clap their hands.

For they hear about the vine,
Growing by the castled Rhine,
Flowing through a land of wine ;

Orange groves and olive trees,
Hanging o'er enchanted seas,
And of fairer things than these ;

Giant palm-leaves waving fair ;
Fragrant figs that fill the air
With an odour rich and rare.

Thus the balmy South winds blow,
Telling, as they come and go,
Of the thousand trees they know.

But the angry East has tales
All of storms and ships in gales;
Broken masts and tattered sails.

And it swirls and shrieks, and breaks
Frightened twigs away, and shakes
Branches till the great trunk quakes.

But the North wind, when it blows,
Tells of ice in bergs and floes;
Bears and seals and Esquimaux.

And it speaks of wondrous sights,
When the magic northern lights
Flare across its Arctic nights.

To the green leaves as they hear,
Shivering with a boding fear
Of the winter drawing near,

Comes the West, and whispers low,
" Leaves and flowers shall not know
Anything of frost and snow."

WHAT THE LEAVES SAY

And it calls the birds to sing
Songs of summer, songs of spring,
Till the widest woodlands ring.

Then the leaves all dance and play;
Every branch and twig and spray,
Calling to the West wind, "Stay!"

I have listened and I've heard
What the leaves say, every word
Like the chirping of a bird.

FANCIES & PICTURES

THE EYES OF GOD.

THE EYES OF GOD.

GOD watches o'er us all the day,
     At home, at school, and at our play;
And when the sun has left the skies
He watches with a million eyes.

THE door was shut, as doors should be,
    Before you went to bed last night;
Yet Jack Frost has got in you see,
    And left your window silver white.

He must have waited till you slept;
    And not a single word he spoke,
But pencilled o'er the panes and crept
    Away again before you woke.

JACK FROST

And now you cannot see the trees
   Nor fields that stretch beyond the lane;
But there are fairer things than these
   His fingers traced on every pane.

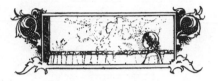

Rocks and castles towering high;
   Hills and dales and streams and fields;
And knights in armour riding by,
   With nodding plumes and shining shields.

And here are little boats, and there
   Big ships with sails spread to the breeze;
And yonder, palm trees waving fair
   On islands set in silver seas.

And butterflies with gauzy wings;
   And herds of cows and flocks of sheep;
And fruit and flowers and all the things
   You see when you are sound asleep.

JACK FROST

For, creeping softly underneath
  The door when all the lights are out,
Jack Frost takes every breath you breathe
  And knows the things you think about.

He paints them on the the window pane
  In fairy lines with frozen steam ;
And when you wake you see again
  The lovely things you saw in dream.

A QUEER THING

WHEN I go to bed, if the night is fine,
    I should like to sit up late;
But in the morning I'd lie till nine
    When mother calls me at eight.

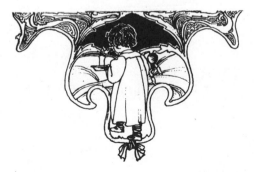

THIS is how the flowers grow:
   I have watched them and I know.

HOW THE FLOWERS GROW

First, above the ground is seen
A tiny blade of purest green,
Reaching up and peeping forth
East and West, and South and North.

North, towards the hills it looks,
To see the silver flash of brooks ;
And it questions of the East
    the winter winds have ceased.

Turning South, it asks the sun
If the springtime has begun ;
From the West it seeks to know
When its warmer winds will blow

Then it shoots up day by day,
Curling in a curious way
Round a blossom, which it keeps
Warm and cosy while it sleeps.

For, although the sun be bright,
Jack Frost walks abroad at night;
And tender buds would surely die
If they were out when Jack went by.

But when birds begin to sing
Of the balmy breath of spring;
And the clouds in summer's quest
All come sailing from the West;

Then the sunbeams find their way
To the sleeping bud and say,
"We are children of the sun
Sent to wake thee, little one."

And the leaflet opening wide
Shows the tiny bud inside,
Peeping with half-opened eye
On the bright and sunny sky.

HOW THE FLOWERS GROW

Breezes from the West and South
Lay their kisses on its mouth ;
Till the petals all are grown,
And the bud's a flower full-blown.

That is how the flowers grow :
I have watched them and I know.

SABBATH DAYS.

I LIKE the Summer Sabbath days;
    For father takes us out a walk
Along the Banks or East the Braes;
    And always of the flowers we talk.

We find a snug and cosy nook,
    Where you might sit for hours and hours;
And father reads us from a book,
    What poets write about the flowers.

SABBATH DAYS

We hear the gowan's poet make
  A song about his bonny gem;
They smile around, and for his sake
  We stay our hands from pulling them.

And flowers that grow in wood and wold;
  On hill and heath, on bank and bent;
We hear one call them, "Blue and gold,
  Stars shining in earth's firmament."

He shuts the book; and then we hear
  How fays and fairies sleep all day
In cradle blooms; till, tinkling clear,
  The dew-drops call them out to play.

Of rounds and fairy rings, he tells,
  When beetles drone and glow-worms glow;
Till we hear the chime of the heather bells
  And a thousand bind-weed bugles blow.

SPRINGTIME.

SING a song of springtime;
   Sing of March and May
When the sun is climbing
  Higher every day;
Wakening and warming
  All the icy earth;
From the clay clods charming
  Flowers into birth;

SPRINGTIME

Hanging hawthorn hedges
   With a bloom of snow;
Kissing woodland edges;
   Bidding violets grow.
Wheresoe'er he lays his
   Light in golden bars,
Buttercups and daisies
   Gleam like suns and stars;

Tender-eyed primroses
   From their clustering leaves
Leap to life in posies,
   Ranked around like sheaves.
And where gorse is gilding
   Bushes bare and brown,
Birds are busy building
   Quite a little town.
Now it's wool they're bringing;
   Moss and straw and hay;
Songs of gladness singing
   All the happy day.

SPRINGTIME

Sing a song of springtime;
  Sing of April showers;
Sing of golden butterflies
  And birds and bees and flowers.

THE COWARD NETTLE

I SAW a bumble bee to-day
  Alight on a nettle leaf;
And when he had rested and buzzed away
  He was not buzzing in grief.

THE COWARD NETTLE

"The nettle did not sting, you see,"
  I said to mother and nurse;
"For the nettle knows if he stung the bee,
  The bee would sting him worse."

The coward nettles only sting
  The hands that are soft and small,
For the gardener grips them like anything
  And they don't hurt him at all.

RAIN IN SPRING

So soft and gentle falls the rain,
   You cannot hear it on the pane;
For if it came in pelting showers,
'Twould hurt the budding leaves and flowers.

FLOWERS from clods of clay and mud !
    Flowers so bright, and grass so green !
Tell me, blade, and leaf, and bud,
    How it is you're all so clean.

A MYSTERY

If my fingers touch these sods,
  See, they're streaked with sticky earth;
Yet you spring from clayey clods,
  Pure, and fresh, and fair from birth.

Do you wash yourselves at night,
  In a bath of diamond dew,
That you look so fresh and bright
  When the morning dawns on you?

God, perhaps, sends summer showers,
  When the grass grows grey for rain,
To wash the faces of His flowers,
  And bid His fields be green again.

A MYSTERY

Tell me, blade, and leaf, and bud;
   Flowers so fair, and grass so green,
Growing out of clay and mud,
   How it is you're all so clean.

 OWS in the meadow
And birds in the
tree ;

ORSES on highways
And fish in the
sea;

 AILORS in
schooners,
And miners in
mines,

 EEP down in pits
where
The sun never
shines;

 IRLS playing jin-go-
ring;
Boys sounding
tops;

107

GOD'S WORK

OTHERS in
kitchens,
And fathers in
shops;

HE sun in the
heavens,
From morning to
night,

AKING the fields
and flowers
Laugh in his
light;

ATCHING o'er
everything
All the day
through;

GOD'S WORK

O WHAT a lot of
work
God has to do!

.DREAMS.

IF children have been good all day,
  And kept their tongues and lips quite clean,
They dream of flowers that nod and play,
  And fairies dancing on the green.

110

DREAMS

But if they've spoken naughty words,
  Or told a lie, they dream of rats;
Of crawling snakes, and ugly birds;
  Of centipedes, and vampire bats.

OH, out in the golden harvest field,
    How pretty the men and women look,
Reaping and winding, lifting and binding!
    It's just like a picture you see in a book.

IN THE HARVEST-FIELD

The reaper wheels are whirring loud;
The coupled horses prancing proud;
The driver swings the rake around;
The ripe grain falls with a sighing sound;
And men and women walk behind,
Some to gather and some to bind;
Till sheaves, like partners, row on row,
Stand waiting the sweep of the fiddle-bow.

So up and down, with faces brown,
    All in their broad-brimmed hats of straw,
Reaping and winding, lifting and binding !
    A prettier picture you never saw.

ON the beach when the tide is out,
   The people meet and walk about;
And boys and girls come, spade in hand,
To make great burrows in the sand.

114

ON THE BEACH

Wherefore the tide comes twice a day
To wash the footprints all away,
And leave the sand so smooth and clean,
You could not tell where holes had been.

And that is how the soft sea sand
Is not all ups and downs like land,
Where rough and sharp-edged stones are found,
While the pebbles here are smooth and round.

I'VE read of children—very sad,
 Who live, and not because they're bad,
In houses where they do not hear
The birdies sing through all the year.

CITY SPARROWS

They've lots of sparrows, but, poor thing,
The sparrow cannot really sing.
He only chirps, and twits, and tweets,
And all because he lives in streets.

For if he came and built his nest,
As all the singing birds find best,
In hedge or field, ere very long
He would have learned to sing a song.

117

CITY SPARROWS

So these poor children have not heard
The songs of any singing bird.
And they can only hear in dreams,
The pebbly murmuring of streams.

Nor have they seen the round sun rise,
All dripping in the eastern skies;
Nor seen him sinking in the west,
Behind the purple hills to rest.

The colliers coming from the pit,
Seek out a sunny place to sit;
But big-town streets are built so high,
They shut the sunshine from the sky.

Could God not take these girls and boys
Away from all the din and noise
Of sunless streets, and set them where
They would not breathe in smoke for air?

Here, in the fields they'd romp and run,
To hear the birds and see the sun;
Till God would clap His hands and shout,
To see His children run about.

THE

SLEEPING

WORLD.

THE SLEEPING WORLD.

THE earth has fallen fast asleep—
    Hills and fields beyond the lane;
And the night has happed them deep,
    In a snowy counterpane.

A PORTRAIT

JOHN MALCOLM was the only man
    The biggest boys in the first class feared;
We gathered up our stakes and ran,
    Whene'er we saw his grisly beard.

For, if we played at marble-holes
    In Malcolm's pend—the grandest place,
He'd creep out on his stocking soles
    To fright us with his hairy face.

A PORTRAIT

He didn't speak, but looked so dark
  And fierce at us, we couldn't play;
Just like a dog that doesn't bark,
  But bites behind, and runs away.

Yet, when I lay so ill in bed,
  John Malcolm came up every night,
To ask me what the doctor said
  And if I had been sleeping right.

At last I could sit up a while;
  And when he brought a shilling ball,
And books and toys, I saw him smile,
  And thought it wasn't John at all.

How kind it was to bring me toys!
  But do you know what mother said?
That John had once two little boys
  Like Rob and me; but they are dead.

CADDIE

CADDIE'S a dog of gentle ways;
    He loves a quiet life, and stays
Indoors on cold and rainy days.

He curls himself up on a chair,
His wee legs hidden anywhere;
You only see a mass of hair.

124

CADDIE

But speak his name, and then he'll rise
And look, with calm and steady eyes,
Through tangled locks, supremely wise.

And when poor Caddie sits and blinks
Before the fire, I know he thinks
Of happy days on northern links.

For that is where he used to stay;
And still at times he hies away,
And sees in dream the golfers play.

ROMANCE

ROMANCE.

I SAW a ship a-sailing,
  A-sailing on the sea;
Her masts were of the shining gold,
  Her deck of ivory;
And sails of silk, as soft as milk,
  And silvern shrouds had she.

129

And round about her sailing,
  The sea was sparkling white,
The waves all clapped their hands and sang
  To see so fair a sight.
They kissed her twice, they kissed her thrice,
  And murmured with delight.

Then came the gallant captain,
  And stood upon the deck;
In velvet coat, and ruffles white,
  Without a spot or speck;
And diamond rings, and triple strings
  Of pearls around his neck.

ROMANCE

And four-and-twenty sailors
  Were round him bowing low;
On every jacket three times three
  Gold buttons in a row;
And cutlasses down to their knees;
  They made a goodly show.

And then the ship went sailing,
  A-sailing o'er the sea;
She dived beyond the setting sun,
  But never back came she,
For she found the lands of the golden sands,
  Where the pearls and diamonds be.

CHIVALRY

U P and down the garden,
    Round the green we ride,
Knights in shining armour
    Keeping side by side;

CHIVALRY

Rob upon a clothes-pole,
  I upon a broom—
Back, ye thorny branches,
  Give our chargers room!
Up and down the garden,
  Round and round the green,
Knights go forth to battle
  For their King and Queen.

Yonder is a castle,
  Where a coward knave
Keeps a lovely princess
  Prisoned like a slave.
"Ho, ye craven hearted,
  Cross a sword with me!"
Soon my trusty blade will
  Bring him to his knee.
From the castle riding
  Back across the green,
We shall bear the princess
  To the King and Queen.

CHIVALRY

Now a band of robbers
   Meets us, ten to one.
Here is work for heroes,
   Ere the day be done.
Spurring on our chargers,
   Hand to hand we fight.
Off go heads of nettles,
   Flying left and right.
Such a crowd of victims
   Scattered o'er the green!
So should knights do battle
   For their King and Queen.

CHIVALRY

But before we rested
  From the bloody fray,
Rob reeled from his charger,
  Threw his sword away;
For a nettle stung him,
  And the pain was sore;
Wounded in the sword hand,
  He could fight no more.
So we left our chargers
  Grazing on the green,
Where we'd battled bravely
  For our King and Queen.

Then we hurried homeward,
  Rob in pain and grief;
And I bound his wound up
  With a docken leaf.
But when mother saw it,
  Blistered, hot, and red,
"Wounded, but not vanquished,"
  That was what she said.
And she told how heroes
  Gloried to have been
Wounded, fighting bravely
  For their King and Queen.

ROBINSON CRUSOE.

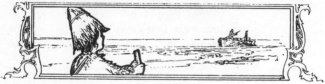

THE tide has turned; the End Rock's bare.
　How fresh its hanging seaweeds show,
Inviting us to wade out there
　And play at Robinson Crusoe!

With knickers pulled above the knees,
　My handkerchief to catch the wind,
I bravely start across the seas,
　And pull my gallant ship behind.

ROBINSON CRUSOE

We leave Rob standing on the beach,
  For he must wait his turn to play;
And, after many dangers, reach
  The island where I'm cast away.

I jump ashore, a prisoner now,
  For here's my gallant bark, a wreck.
The billows break against its prow,
  And seaweed falls across its deck.

Then, first of all, I must explore
  The island; but I see no sign,
Except one print upon the shore
  Of any other foot than mine.

But I discover, clear and cool,
  The sweetest dulse that one could wish,
And whelks and crabs and, in a pool,
  A shoal of shining silver fish.

I build myself a hut close by,
  With roaring buckies, large and white,
Where, through a solen shell, I spy,
  If there be any sail in sight.

Yet silently I move about—
  For crabs and whelks and fish are dumb;
Until my jacket inside out
  Tells Rob on shore it's time to come.

And then at last there comes a noise,
  And not the sound of wind or wave.
I see a face, and hear a voice
  That whispers to me, " White man, save."

And when I've led him to a seat,
  He smacks his lips and asks for food.
I run and fetch him dulse to eat,
  And with his thumb he calls it good.

ROBINSON CRUSOE

But when we see a score of brown,
　　Fierce cannibals upon our shore,
We shoulder guns and shoot them down—
　　And tangles fall to rise no more.

At length we put them all to rout,
　　When Friday, looking to the sea,
Cries, all at once, "The tide is out,"
　　And then we know it's time for tea.

TIME & TIDE ·

A SCHOONER cam' ayont the quay;
    An' oh, she was a sicht to see,
Wi' silken sails an' masts o' gowd;
Her ropes in threeds o' silver row'd!
Oh, sic a bonny ship as this
The waves cam' loupin' keen to kiss!

TIME AND TIDE

The skipper stapped upon the deck,
A gowden chain about his neck,
Wi' strings o' pearlins hanging doun,
An' silver buckles on his shoon.

"Oh, wha shall come an' sail wi' me
To sunny lands ayont the sea,
Whaur skies are o' the cloudless blue,
An' summer bides the twalmonth through.

"Come, sign, an' sail across the main,
Ye'll ne'er hae sic a chance again.
For a better craft there couldna be
Than the 'Gowden Opportunity.'"

SHIPWRECK·

OUR garret has a secret door
    That lies flat down upon the floor;
And when you're up and let it slip,
You'd think you were on board a ship.

SHIPWRECK

So here it is we come and play
At sailors, on a rainy day.
And when we touch at foreign isles,
The raindrops thunder on the tiles.

Three masts our ship has, tall and strong,
With cross-trees all the way along.
We draw the deck in lines of chalk,
That show how far it's safe to walk.

I am the skipper, because I know
The ports where all the big ships go;
And Rob is mate, and climbs the mast
To speak the steamers sailing past.

Jack-in-the-box and a wooden horse
Are men before the mast, of course;
May's doll is cook—her second best—
With empty reels for all the rest.

SHIPWRECK

Then Rob astride the cross-trees cries,
His hand held out above his eyes:
"There's rocks upon the weather bow.
Too late, too late! She's on them now."

And when our gallant ship's a wreck,
We haul the chests about the deck.
Then falling down upon the floor,
We swim until we reach the shore.

There, sitting down to count the crew,
We find that all are drowned but two.
Of those who sailed across the sea,
There's no one saved but Rob and me.

FAIRYLAND

O N a sunny summer day,
      When the very wind was warm,
Little Nellie walked away,
   With a basket on her arm;

Past the fields and through the wood,
   Till she reached an open place,
Where in wonder Nellie stood,
   With the sunlight on her face.

145

FAIRYLAND

For it was a lovely sight
  Nellie saw that summer noon:
Roses red and roses white,
  All the flowers of rosy June.

Daisies from their slender stems
  Gazed up to the glorious sun;
Dewdrops lay like little gems
  In the eyes of every one.

Golden buttercups were there,
  Pinks with kingly coronets;
While the perfume in the air
  Told of hiding violets.

FAIRYLAND

Grass and trees were fresh and green,
  Blossoms white and red and blue;
Flowers that she had never seen,
  Fairer than the flowers she knew.

What a wondrous spot it was,
  Lovelier than tongue can tell!
"Beautiful," she said, "because
  This is where the fairies dwell."

And she heard the birds and bees
  Filling all the air with song;
While a brook among the trees
  Wimpled sweetly all day long.

"Bees, oh, tell me, as you hum,
  Tell me, if you understand—
Have I really, really come
  To the gates of Fairyland?"

FAIRYLAND

But the birds and bees flew by,
  Singing, humming, every one ;
And a golden butterfly
  Fluttered gaily in the sun.

Then a cloud rose slowly up,
  Roses sighed and winds grew cold ;
Daisy, pink, and buttercup
  Lost their silver and their gold.

MY VALENTINE

*T*HE *rose is red,*
   The violet's blue.
That's what I've said
   To Cissy Hugh.
For I am ten and she is nine,
And I'm sending her a valentine.

MY VALENTINE

I wrote as neat
  As I could do
The honey's sweet
  And so are you.
And then made crosses in a line,
For kisses on her valentine.

Then must I say
  What none should miss:
And so are they
  Who send you this.
And every word was written fine
Upon her pretty valentine.

And last, how sweet
  To say to Cis,
And when we meet
  We'll have a kiss.
Now I shall write her name and mine,
And take to her my valentine.

MY VALENTINE

But when I got
    To *Cissy from,*
I made a blot
    Instead of *Tom.*
And big tears fell on every line ;
So Cissy lost her valentine.

TO ROB AND MAY.

DEAR May, you're quite a lady now,
       Of quiet speech and placid brow.
But still I look and recognise
The May of childhood in your eyes.
And so your eyes may read my rhymes,
And see again those happy times,
When skies were always bright and clear,
And days of sunshine filled the year.

155

TO ROB AND MAY

And Rob, who sailed to other lands,
But never found the golden sands
We saw in dream in bygone days,
May stumble on them in these lays;
Then close the book and play with me
A dream-span by our sunny sea.

TO
BESSIE

I AM gathering up to take a trip
    To London Town, to London Town.
The cheapest way is to go by ship
    To far-away London Town.
But quicker it is to go by rail;
So steaming away o'er hill and dale,
I shall speed as fast as the Royal Mail
    To famous London Town.

TO BESSIE

I cannot come whenever I will
      To London Town, to London Town,
Or I'd stand to-morrow on Denmark Hill,
      In far-away London Town.
For, oh, it's there that I fain would be!
Where a little lass that I long to see
Is watching and waiting to welcome me
      To famous London Town.

But I'm coming up to print a book
      In London Town, in London Town;
That will bring the songs of bird and brook
      To far-away London Town.
And when it comes from the printing press
I'll send it straight to the good Queen Bess:
And Denmark Hill is my Queen's address,
      In famous London Town.

TO BESSIE

And she shall read her name in verse
      In London Town, in London Town;
And the names of little friends of hers
      Far away from London Town.
But when I come I mustn't miss
A great reward for doing this—
A kiss of greeting and a good-bye kiss
      From Bessie in London Town.

TO
MAY
AND
MARY.

DEAR May and Mary, here's a book
    Of songs for little boys and girls,
Where older folks in vain may look
    For grains of gold or goodly pearls.
For grown-up people, being dull,
    Will only see the lines and words,
Where bright-eyed little ones may cull
    The flowers and hear the songs of birds

160

And so I send this book to you,
  Whose hearts are pure, whose eyes are clear;
And when you've read it through and through
  You'll find your own names printed here.
And one of you will criticise,
  And pick and choose and pass and praise;
The other one, with dreamy eyes,
  Will see a world of summer days.

TO MAY AND MARY

And in your cosy bed at night
   The one will hear my songs in bars
Of music; while on wings of light
   The other glides among the stars;
And on, and on, and on, she'll float,
   Until she reach the Milky Way,
Returning in a moonbeam boat,
   And wakening on the rim of day.

TO

AUNTIE

D EAR Auntie, in the afternoon,
   When you sit down to read and rest,
Perchance you'll hear the embers croon
   The rhymes of mine you liked the best;

TO AUNTIE

Until you close your eyes in dreams,
    And see some far-off August morn,
Two little lads who trudge from Wemyss,
    To stay with Auntie in Kinghorn.

TO THE

BOYS OF BARNCRAIG.
(*(Wemyss.)*

A LONG the old familiar shore
I walked as in the days gone by,
And heard the waves sing as of yore,
When life was young and hopes were high.

165

TO THE BOYS OF BARNCRAIG

And through the links the footpath wound,
   Unchanged as to our boyhood's feet,
Beyond the Lady's Rock, and round
   The caves and down to Milly's seat,

Where children climb and romp and race,
   And every one comes to recall
A far-away, familiar face,
   Though I'm a stranger to them all.

They play their games with rules, and rhymes
   From other days and other boys;
I hear a clinking phrase at times,
   And start to recognise the voice.

So resting here, I see again
   A score of schoolboys trudging by;
And hear them laugh and shout, as when
   They played with Time and let it fly.

They march away to war in fun,
   Behind a ragged lad, who looks
A hero in the eyes of one
   Who tells them stories out of books.

TO THE BOYS OF BARNCRAIG

I see the cannon where we played
  At soldiers, when we beat the Czar;
The wreck still lies where once we made
  Our gallant fight at Trafalgar.

There Nelson led us in the fight,
  And swung his books around his head;
Then hurling them with all his might,
  He left a hundred Frenchmen dead.

And heedless of his boots and socks,
  He plunged into the dub and chased
The flying ships against the rocks,
  Until the water touched his waist.

The years go by; I watch them still,
  And see how thin our ranks have grown.
For one by one they go, until
  I'm left to trudge the road alone.

TO THE BOYS OF BARNCRAIG

For they had lives to live, and went
  To pit and bench, to board and stool;
But I'd to live in books, and spent
  The wasted years of youth at school.

Now, thinking of you all to-day,
  And of your full and healthy lives,
I see in dream your children play,
  And hear the prattle of your wives.

And if at all you think of him
  Who once was of you, or at times,
Perchance, when day is growing dim,
  Remember snatches of his rhymes;

Then call your children round, and read
  Some verses from these simple lays,
And so perhaps they'll win the meed
  He cannot find them—childhood's praise.

For you have wives with smiling looks,
  And happy children all your own;
But he who told you tales from books
  Lives in his book-world yet, alone.

TO ALL
CHILDREN

D EAR children, living everywhere,
     In country lane, in street, or square,
I would that I might take your hand,
And lead you into Fairyland,
Where life is all a sunny day,
And summer lasts from May to May;
Where woods and fields are green and fair,
And songs of gladness fill the air;
For birds and flowers and everything
That lives has got a song to sing.

TO ALL CHILDREN

And here three little children dwell,
Far happier than tongue can tell;
Through wood and vale and field they roam,
For Fairyland is all their home.
The birds come to them when they call,
And lambs and sheep, they know them all;
And winds and trees and bays and brooks
These children have for lesson books.
Oh, joyous is the life they spend,
Where every flower is their friend.

Oh, children, I would take your hand,
And lead you to that Fairyland;
Where childhood's still a world of dream,
With songs of bird and wind and stream.
And should you read this book and stay
Where those three happy children play,
Though only for an hour it be,
The book will bless both you and me.

A CHILD'S GARDEN of VERSES

BY ROBERT LOVIS STEVENSON

ILLVSTRATED BY CHARLES ROBINSON.

SHAMBHALA
BOULDER
1979

LULLABY LAND.

Songs of Childhood,

by

EUGENE FIELD.

Selected by KENNETH
GRAHAME, and
illustrated by CHARLES
ROBINSON.

18 97

SHAMBHALA
BOULDER
1979